Other books by Wilferd A. Peterson

THE ART OF LIVING (1961)
THE NEW BOOK OF THE ART OF LIVING (1963)

MORE ABOUT
THE ART

OF LIVING

A THIRD BOOK OF 25 NEW ESSAYS

by WILFERD A. PETERSON

SIMON AND SCHUSTER   NEW YORK

Acknowledgments

My thanks to my friend Cornell W. Lugthart, the man who repainted the angel (see p. 18), and to all others who have aided me in my search for inspiration on the arts of living. My thanks to Chester A. Jaqua, founder of the advertising firm The Jaqua Company, who opened the way for me to become a writer; to Ray Strindmo of Bermingham & Prosser Company, who first had the idea of putting my essays in a book; to William I. Nichols, publisher of This Week Magazine, *who gave my essays an audience of many millions of readers; and to Henry W. Simon and my publishers for their encouragement and help. My special thanks to my wife, Ruth Rector Peterson, who has worked with me on each essay and whose counsel and guidance have been invaluable to me.*

Introduction

THE ART OF

THIS IS *my third book of Art of Living essays.*

As in the other two books, each essay explores in depth a vital phase of living. Each endeavors to condense the wisdom of many thinkers. But on subjects on which many volumes have been written these brief essays do not profess to do more than stimulate and inspire further thinking. Ideally, they are a starting point for your own thought.

You can easily read this little book through in an evening, but if you do, I hope you will return to it many times, to read slowly and thoughtfully, one essay each time.

Since the first two books appeared, I have received many letters telling me about the various ways the books are being used.

Some readers find it helpful to keep the books on the bedside table and to read an essay each night before going to sleep.

Others read an essay each morning and find that it sets up their minds encouragingly for the activities of the day.

GETTING THE MOST
OUT OF THIS BOOK

Still others have made the reading of the Art of Living books a family affair. Each evening, after dinner, the members of the family take turns reading an essay aloud. This is often followed by a family discussion of the essay.

Service clubs and other organizations have used the reading of an essay aloud as a way to get meetings off to an inspirational start.

Study groups have based their programs for an entire year on a selected Art of Living essay for each meeting, with a leader who gathers additional data on the subject of the essay and leads the discussion.

This widening circle of use of the essays is gratifying to me. It indicates that the books are not being read and forgotten but that they are being lived with and remembered . . . that readers are finding the books helpful in their continuing efforts to make living an art.

WILFERD A. PETERSON

1721 Woodward Avenue, S. E.
Grand Rapids, Michigan

*It is with words as with sunbeams . . .
the more they are condensed, the deeper
they burn.*

—ROBERT SOUTHEY

Contents

The Art of

Each day is a lifetime in miniature.

To awaken each morning is to be born again, to fall asleep at night is to die to the day.

In between waking and sleeping are the golden hours of the day.

What we cannot do for a lifetime we can do for a *daytime*.

"Anyone," wrote Robert Louis Stevenson, "can live sweetly, patiently, lovingly, purely, till the sun goes down."

Anyone can hold his temper for a day and guard the words he speaks.

Anyone can carry his burden heroically for one day.

Anyone can strive to be happy for a day and to spread happiness around.

Anyone can radiate love for a day.

Anyone can rise above fear for a day and meet each situation with courage.

LIVING EACH DAY

Anyone can be kind and thoughtful and considerate for a day.

Anyone can endeavor to learn something new each day and mark some growth.

Sir William Osler pointed out that just as ships are kept afloat by airtight compartments, living in daytight compartments will help us avoid wrecking our lives. Osler gives us a magic word with which to face the day: *Equanimity*.

The supreme art of living is to strive to live each day well.

When we fail and fall short, let us forgive ourselves and consider the words of Emerson: "Finish every day and be done with it. You have done what you could; some blunders and absurdities have crept in; forget them as soon as you can. Tomorrow is a new day; you will begin it well and serenely and with too high a spirit to be cumbered by your old nonsense."

Live a day at a time and remember that tomorrow is another *today*.

The Art of

The art of becoming rich is simply to live richly in body, mind, heart and spirit.

You become physically rich when you have rich sensations: When your senses are alert and attuned to life so that the very fact of being alive takes on new dimensions and simple experiences have new meaning . . . the smell of a rose, the stretch of a muscle, the sight of a mountain, the sound of the surf, the taste of strawberries, the touch of clean white sheets . . .

You become mentally rich when you think rich thoughts: When you immerse your mind in the noble thoughts of men, preserved through the ages in books; when you are curious to learn all you can about the world and its people, the earth beneath your feet and the farthest star in infinite space; when you develop an appreciation of beauty in painting and sculpture, poetry and music; when you expand your mind to encompass great ideas;

BECOMING RICH

when you use the magic of your mind to create and to serve . . .

You become emotionally rich when you have rich feelings: When you know the radiant glow of obeying noble impulses to give and help and inspire; when you experience the bond of warm friendship and deep affection; when you know the joy of hearing a baby laugh; when you are aware of giving and receiving love . . .

You become spiritually rich when you discover the riches of the kingdom within: When you have a consciousness of the oneness of all life; when you experience kinship with nature; when you are open to the buoyant spiritual lift of being in tune with the Infinite; when you know the power of meditation and prayer.

The best definition of a rich man is a man with a rich self. What a man *is*, not what he has, is the measure of real wealth.

The Art of

The statuette of an angel holding the hand of a little boy had been placed on a neglected back shelf in an antique shop. It was covered with soot and dust, lost amidst the clutter of jars, dishes and ornaments.

A man browsing through the shop discovered the figurine and took it in his hands. He had an inspiration! He would rescue it from oblivion, restore it, and give it a place of honor among his Christmas decorations.

At home, in his basement workshop, the man covered the angel and the child with glistening white paint. Then he painted the wings of the angel and the hair of the little boy with sparkling gold. Each brush stroke worked magic. The old grime-covered statuette vanished and a shining new one appeared. The statuette was transformed before his eyes into a thing of radiant beauty.

As the man painted, he thought: "Isn't this what happens to people at Christmas? They come to the end of the year dust-covered from the struggle. And then Christmas inspires them

REPAINTING
THE ANGEL

to repaint the better angels of their natures with love and joy and peace.''

The art of repainting the angel! This is man's lifelong task. Never to stay down in the dust and the dirt. Heroically to rise again after each fall. To create a new life.

Repainting the angel! There is a hidden goodness within every man, and he has the power to bring it forth.

Repainting the angel! A man need never lose his ideals, dreams and purposes. He can always make them gleam again with the glory of renewed hope.

Repainting the angel! A man always has another chance to restore the image of his best self, to regain lost ground, to start over again.

Repainting the angel! Each high thought a man thinks works magic. It helps to transform him and renew his spirit. Just as gold paint will change a statuette, golden thoughts will change a man.

19

The Art of

A home should be a stockade, a refuge from the flaming arrows of anxiety, tension and worry.

An old art needs to be rediscovered: the art of staying home, the renewing power of love and joy and peace within the home.

Stay home to gather the family together. Let dinnertime be a time of candlelight, music and conversation, serious and gay. Share a great thought and discuss it. Say a prayer of thankfulness for your blessings.

Stay home to read those books you've long intended to read. From your comfortable chair you can send your mind forth on adventure around the world. Discover the pleasure of reading aloud.

Stay home to meditate. Get away by yourself in a quiet room where you can think, undisturbed, about yourself and your destiny. A wise man has said: "We can only be ourselves if we are often enough by ourselves."

Stay home to have fun. Play games in which all can join. Make the house ring with laughter.

20

STAYING HOME

Stay home to let go. Drop your cares. Learn the satisfaction of doing as you please. Let time slip by without a thought of the future.

Stay home to find beauty. Open your eyes to a new appreciation of your surroundings: the furniture, the wallpaper, the pictures on the walls, the woodwork, the view from a window, the flowers in the garden . . . Open yourself to a new awareness of the love in the faces of those with whom your home is shared.

Stay home to relive the past. Revive precious memories. Look at old photographs. Your wedding. Baby pictures of the children. Seek out again the treasures that bind you together as a family.

Stay home to find happiness. Realize the wisdom of simplicity.

Stay home to search for inspiration. Browse through the works of great thinkers, prophets and sages to lift your sights and broaden your vision.

Stay home to prepare for tomorrow, that you may go forth as a new person, with a new spirit, to meet triumphantly the challenges of the outside world.

The Art of

Revolution is the process of drastic change.

Sometimes there is the need of *personal revolution* within ourselves.

In a personal revolution you are your own enemy and self-conquest is your goal.

A personal revolution is a revolt against wrong, despondent, hopeless thinking.

It is a bold offensive to change habits, thought patterns, actions, and establish a new way of life.

It is an about-face. It is turning a corner, taking a new road, moving in a new direction.

It is breaking the bonds of slavery to the past so that you may walk in freedom.

It is implanting creative and constructive thoughts in your mind, to destroy the weeds of negative thinking.

REVOLUTION

It is sweeping away the decaying foundations of your life that stronger and more enduring ones may be laid for you to build upon.

It is smashing destructive idols and images and gaining a new vision of the person you would become.

It is shaking yourself awake, coming alive, re-establishing your hopes and dreams.

It is waging a battle against complacency, self-satisfaction and inertia. It is stopping drift. It is grabbing the oars and rowing with purpose.

It is overcoming the failure complex by beginning to act as though you cannot fail.

It is a declaration of independence from all that would drag you down, and it is reaching out for all that will lift you up.

It is overthrowing fear and putting faith on the throne.

23

The Art of

The art of courtesy is the practice of the Golden Rule in little things.

It is being courteous even to those who are discourteous. It is striving to avoid a reaction of irritation in spite of the most severe provocation. It is remembering that "a soft answer turneth away wrath."

It is coming forward to meet others with warmth, graciousness and a hospitable spirit.

It is using shock-absorber words to smooth the jars and jolts of daily living; words that express kindness, consideration and gratitude.

It is the wisdom to know that we should love before we think and think before we act.

It is putting people at ease, helping them to relax. It is recognizing the worth of the individual, protecting his dignity, inspiring him to think well of himself.

COURTESY

It is the sympathetic ear and the understanding heart.

It is going the second mile to make things pleasant for others.

It is appreciating what others do for us and letting them know it.

It is being big enough to take the blame for our mistakes and being quick to ask forgiveness for our blunders.

It is recognizing the universal power of a smile; for a sincere smile is courtesy in *every language* and puts a glow in the heart everywhere on earth.

It is emphasizing the *gentle* in gentleman.

It is endeavoring to live with some nobility that we may prove that the age of chivalry isn't dead.

It is keeping constantly in mind the words of Emerson: "Life is not so short but that there is always time enough for courtesy."

The Art of

There is no life without tension. Evolution is the story of stress and conflict, change and adjustment—the unconquerable urge of life to emerge in new forms.

The philosophy of "easy does it" meets no challenge, records no progress.

Man does not win a race, climb a mountain, write a book, give a speech, paint a picture, develop an invention, found a business, or do anything that matters without tension. Tension quickens the senses, alerts mind and body.

Tension is man on tiptoe reaching for the stars. Tension is the fire of the spirit, the thirst for achievement, the surge of dynamic energy.

Tension is your friend. It is concern, excitement, stimulation, drive. It is you mobilized, applying the best that is in you to the task before you. It is all of your powers organized and concentrated for victory.

Tension has its evil side. When extreme and sustained it often kills. Extreme rest and ease, on the other hand, deadens initi-

TENSION

ative and extinguishes the creative spark. The secret is this: *Balance tension with rest.*

The Master of men withdrew to mountain, desert and lake to rest, meditate and renew his spirit that he might return with new strength to His great work. He said: "Come ye apart into a desert place and rest awhile."

Every man needs a place of retreat . . . his own Walden Pond. Thus he recharges himself, so he can be tense again in a good cause!

Tension and relaxation can be instantly balanced even in the midst of action. Close your eyes for a moment and fly away from tension on the wings of imagination . . . see yourself on the shores of a quiet lake or walking through a sunny meadow. A wise scientist counsels: "Use your moments of unavoidable delay to relax and build up your energy reserves."

By alternating tension and relaxation you balance pressure and release, outgo and intake, giving and receiving, expending and renewing.

Not tension *alone*, not relaxation *alone*, but both in balance is the key to creative living.

The Art of

The well-known maxim, "While there is life there is hope," has deeper meaning in reverse: *"While there is hope there is life."*

Hope comes first, life follows. Hope gives power to life. Hope rouses life to continue, to expand, to grow, to reach out, to go on.

Hope sees a light where there isn't any. Hope lights candles in millions of despairing hearts.

Hope is the miracle medicine of the mind. It inspires the will to live. Hope is the physician's strongest ally.

Hope is man's shield and buckler against defeat. "Hope," wrote Alexander Pope, "springs eternal in the human breast." And as long as it does man will triumph and move forward.

Hope never sounds retreat. Hope keeps the banners flying.

HOPE

Hope revives ideals, renews dreams, revitalizes visions.

Hope scales the peak, wrestles with the impossible, achieves the highest aim.

Hope discovered America. In the face of unknown seas and the terror of a mutinous crew, Columbus gave the command of hope: "Sail on! Sail on and on!"

Hope, alone, remained in Pandora's box after all other blessings had escaped. Greek mythology thus proclaims hope as the indispensable blessing of life.

"The word which God has written on the brow of every man," wrote Victor Hugo, "is Hope."

As long as a man has hope no situation is hopeless.

When you reach the end of your rope, use hope to tie a knot in it—and hang on!

The Art of

The art of forgiveness begins when you forgive someone.

It is having a humble spirit and being done with pride and self-pity. It is taking a step toward the practice of forgiveness. Hate is death, forgiveness is life.

Forgiveness works the miracle of change. When Lincoln was asked why he did not destroy his enemies he replied: "If I make my enemies my friends, don't I then destroy them?" When you forgive you change others and you change yourself. You change discord to harmony.

Forgiveness should span the years. You should first forgive yourself for the wrongs you've done to yourself and others, for the mistakes you've made. Then you should forgive and bless all those who have wronged you during your lifetime. Thus you release others and you release yourself. You break the chains of regret and remorse that bind you. You free your mind from the burdens of the past so you may walk victoriously into the future.

FORGIVENESS

Forgiveness works two ways. You must forgive to be forgiven. "He who cannot forgive others," wrote Edward Herbert, "breaks the bridge over which he himself must pass; for every man has the need to be forgiven."

Forgiveness should become a habit. When the Master was asked how often we should forgive, he answered: "Until seventy times seven." He who forgives to infinity will never hate.

Forgiveness should start now. Putting off forgiving only deepens the wound. Clinging to bitterness postpones happiness. Life is short, time is fleeting. Today is the day to forgive.

Forgiveness is the way to personal peace. It is performing mental surgery on yourself, probing deep within to remove hurts, grudges and resentments. It is forgetting wrongs as though they had never been. It is flooding your mind with the powerful medicine of forgiveness that cleanses and heals. It is discovering a serenity you've never known before.

The Art of

The art of humility begins with a recognition of our dependence on others and an appreciation of God's gift of life.

A man becomes humble when he sees himself in imagination standing naked, helpless and alone at the dawn of man's creation.

When he realizes that millions of men, in thousands of battles, have given their lives to make him free.

When he is aware of the enormous debt he owes to others who have labored through the ages to fashion the world he lives in. When he acknowledges that he is the heir of infinite riches he did not create.

When he considers how little he knows of all there is to know. When he understands how the philosopher Will Durant felt, when he wrote on his seventy-fifth birthday: "I feel like a drop of water trying to understand the ocean."

When he stands under the stars at night and meditates on his insignificance compared with the vast reaches of the universe.

When he measures his inadequacy in the face of the multitude of undone tasks that face mankind.

HUMILITY

When he ponders the miracle of his own body, which, without his conscious thought, controls heartbeat and respiration, digests food, compounds chemicals, renews cells, combats disease, heals wounds, maintaining the equilibrium of his intricate physical being.

Out of such contemplation a man becomes truly humble.

Because he knows so little about so much he becomes teachable, open-minded and flexible. He never stops growing.

Because he realizes his own limitations he becomes more tolerant and understanding of others.

Because he is grateful for the immeasurable contributions others have made to his life he is not blinded by arrogance and pride. He has greater vision because his ego does not get in his way.

He discovers that those of a gentle spirit *do* have the earth for their possession; that humility opens the gates of the mind and heart so greatness can flow through.

The Art of

Ideas are the beginning of all things.

The world we live in today first existed as ideas in the minds of men . . . bridges, skyscrapers, automobiles, airplanes, religions, philosophies, governments, symphonies, paintings, poems . . . *everything!*

Man's future is vast because God has given him unlimited power to create ideas. Man's greatest freedom is freedom to think.

Man's mind has immense scope. "The mind," wrote Lewis Mumford, "is a power station, a storage warehouse, a library, a theatre, a museum, a hall of archives, a court of justice, a seat of government."

Ideas make men giants. The art of creating ideas is man's most challenging quest . . .

First, a man must win the battle against his own inertia. "There is no expedient to which man will not resort to avoid the real labor of thinking," wrote Joshua Reynolds.

Second, he will learn from Edison, who said, "I am more of a sponge than an inventor." He will sponge up all the data and

CREATING IDEAS

facts about a problem, look at it from every angle, attack it with power and penetration.

Third, he will harness the power of his subconscious mind. When intense concentration on the conscious level fails to reveal the answer, he will relax, play golf, fish, listen to music, or sleep on the problem. He will use what Oliver Wendell Holmes called "the underground workshop of the mind."

Fourth, he will keep alert to the stream of thought continuously flowing through his mind. Like a prospector panning for gold, he will watch for the idea-nuggets that flash in his consciousness.

Fifth, he will evaluate the ideas he receives. He will reject the inferior ones and polish and improve the good ones.

Sixth, he will turn ideas from dreams into realities. He will make them servants of man.

Millions of ideas are awaiting discovery by the minds of men . . . ideas that will change the world, build the peace, conquer man's common enemies.

Every man can contribute more if he will think more.

The Art of

He who would practice the art of tolerance must guard well against an attitude of superiority, smugness, indifference and coldness. These qualities are tolerance turned wrong side out!

Tolerance is warm. It reaches out the hand of friendship in spite of all differences.

Tolerance is understanding. It is open to new light. He who is tolerant is always eager to explore viewpoints other than his own.

Tolerance is deep. It creates a foundation of faith in humanity underneath disagreements, thus preventing prejudice and resentment. It may reject the argument, but it always respects the man.

Tolerance radiates good will. It disagrees agreeably. It unites men in spirit even though they are a thousand miles apart in their convictions.

TOLERANCE

Tolerance practices fair play. It doesn't force one man's views on another. The tolerant man makes up his own mind and extends to others the same freedom. He agrees with Josh Billings that "the best creed we can have is charity toward the creeds of others."

Tolerance refuses to hate. Booker T. Washington put it well when he said, "I will not permit any man to narrow and degrade my soul by making me hate him."

Tolerance is sympathetic. It looks through mental barriers into the human heart. It agrees with the French proverb: "To comprehend all is to pardon all."

Tolerance does not look down on others, it looks up to them. Henry Van Dyke gave us a golden maxim for tolerance when he wrote: "Live by admiration rather than by disgust. Judge people by their best, not by their worst."

Tolerance towers above differences. It is bigger than race, color, creed, or politics.

The Art of

Common sense is a personal compass for guidance around the rocks and shoals of life.

Common sense is not based on theory; it is not a hypothesis. It is life acted out, it is discoveries made in the crucible of existence. It is the tried and tested experiences of mankind.

Common sense sits in judgment on the centuries, on every science, every religion, every art, every government. It is based on what has been proved true, sound and practical.

Common sense is the voice of the ages. It is the distilled essence of what men have learned about life as expressed in the proverbs and maxims of all nations. "That man is happy who lives on his own labor," observed the Egyptian. "Just scale and full measure injure no man," recorded the Chinese. "Examine what is said and not who speaks," said the Arabian. "An idle brain is the devil's workshop," wrote the English . . .

Common sense is pragmatic. It is what William James called "the cash value of an idea." It is a method that works, a truth that can be applied.

COMMON SENSE

Common sense is the common denominator of intelligence, the key to right answers.

Common sense recognizes the utter senselessness of war, the irrationality of using death, suffering and destruction as a way of settling disputes.

Common sense observes that crime does not pay, that murder will be found out, that the law of compensation works relentlessly and cannot be escaped.

Common sense is the rock on which every enduring institution and organization must be built.

Common sense is the law of God written into the nature of the universe. It is the sum total of the workable findings of man in his long evolution toward the light.

Common sense is dynamic, not static. It changes as time goes on.

The art of common sense is applying the best wisdom we know today based on all our yesterdays.

The Art of

Albert Schweitzer's principal legacy to mankind consists of three words, sealed by a life that was a triumphant example of their power.

At sunset one evening, while journeying up the Ogowe River in Africa, Schweitzer's mind lighted up with a phrase which brought his whole philosophy of life into sharp focus: *Reverence for life*.

As a jungle doctor Schweitzer founded a hospital in Africa which grew from a converted chicken coop into a world-famous institution. Here for half a century Schweitzer practiced his philosophy of reverence for life. He was called "a genius of compassion."

"We are like waves that do not move individually but rise and fall in rhythm," wrote the great man. "To share, to rise and fall in rhythm with life around us is a spiritual necessity."

The phrase *Reverence for life* is simple and direct. It was Schweitzer's fervent hope that though he might be forgotten, these words would live. He wanted others to understand them and use them.

We can make these three dynamic words a part of our lives and practice the art of *Reverence for life* in these ways . . .

By becoming aware that God is the source of all life and that

REVERENCE
FOR LIFE

we are one with life. "The good man," said Schweitzer "is the friend of all living things."

By having reverence for ourselves and our own God-given talents and abilities and dedicating them to helping others. By seeking and finding a work through which we can best contribute to the lives of others. Schweitzer often quoted the Master's secret: "He who loses his life shall find it."

By always reaching out to life, to help life to grow, to express itself, and to fulfill its highest destiny.

By striving to live affirmatively. By looking for the good in life and glorifying it.

By having a deep sense of obligation for the precious gift of life. By giving of ourselves that we may repay life, at least in some small measure, for the infinite treasures it pours at our feet.

By coming to know that *Reverence for life* is the very heart of our relations with our fellow men; that we should reverence each other, recognize that we are a part of each other, and live together in a spirit of love.

By realizing that when we war on life we war on ourselves, and that *Reverence for life* is the only pathway to the Kingdom of Peace and Brotherhood.

The Art of

The art of retirement can be summed up briefly in this way: *Don't retire . . . aspire!*

Retire means to move back, retreat, withdraw.

Aspire means to move forward, to seek the best.

Aspire! Retirement does not mean that you are all through. It means that you have experienced a big *breakthrough* to a new freedom, with the time to do the things you've always wanted to do.

Aspire to make the most of each new day. In the morning think first of the words of the psalmist: "This is the day which the Lord hath made, let us rejoice and be glad in it."

Aspire to widen your horizons. See new people and places. Adventure across America and around the world.

Aspire to serve. Work now for those causes you've always believed in. Lend a hand to worthy organizations and movements.

Aspire to grow. Stretch your mind with the thoughts of great thinkers. Live many lives through the pages of biography. Explore the earth and the stars. Now you have time to read!

Aspire to discover the greatness within yourself that you've never had the time to develop before. Paint, carve, play a

RETIREMENT

musical instrument, invent, write a book, plant a garden . . . *create!*

Aspire to maintain a youthful attitude toward life. Harry Emerson Fosdick said it well: "It is magnificent to grow old if only one stays young."

Aspire to be an inspiration to others. What you are counts more than what you do. Let your light shine. Be a source of strength and courage. Share your wisdom. Radiate love.

Aspire to attain an awareness of the joy of living. Celebrate life! Remember the words of Santayana: "The young man who has not wept is a savage, and the old man who will not laugh is a fool!"

Aspire to realize the power of the spirit. Seek the quietness and solitude for which you have longed. Think and meditate. Be still and know the serenity of inner peace.

Aspire to live all of your life. Rise to the challenge of these words from a letter written by Justice Oliver Wendell Holmes on his ninety-first birthday: "Life seems to me like a Japanese picture which our imagination does not allow to end with the margin. We aim at the infinite and when our arrow falls to earth it is in flames."

Aspire!

The Art of

"The first lesson of History," wrote Emerson, "is the good of evil. Good is a good doctor, but bad is sometimes a better...."

Crisis is creative.

The crisis of the American Revolution created an explosive new idea in government.

The crisis of plagues and epidemics sweeping the world inspired men to create new miracles in medicine.

The crisis of war has spurred men on, not only to create new weapons to destroy, but also to create new methods of saving, preserving and maintaining life and building an enduring peace.

The crisis of adversity has created the resolve and determination to conquer obstacles and has helped to fashion our greatest men.

Out of crisis flow new ideas, new approaches, new patterns, new inventions, new discoveries, new leadership . . .

CRISIS

Crisis is challenge. It can challenge you to create a new life. Out of disappointment and defeat, out of illness and despair you can find victory.

At a time of crisis you face a turning point. You can go either way, up or down, forward or back. Your choice determines your destiny.

Crisis is a test and those who meet it and overcome it become stronger in the process.

Crisis is your chance to meet a problem head-on, wrestle with it and win.

Crisis burns the dross from the gold; crisis refines.

The art of crisis is rising to meet each new crisis with a heroic spirit.

The Art of

Out of a block of ivory, Pygmalion chiseled the form of a beautiful woman, Galatea. As he worked with inspired zeal a miracle happened. Galatea came to life!

Many potentially happy and successful people are imprisoned in the ivory of defeat and despair. You can release them to *new* life through the miracle-working power of your inspiring influence.

"One single ray of light," wrote Arnold Bennett, "one single precious hint, will clarify and energize the whole mental life of him who receives it."

Work miracles with praise. Appreciation accelerates accomplishment. Men go on to bigger things when they are made to feel that their work is worthwhile.

Work miracles by painting visions. Help men to see themselves as the men they can become.

Work miracles by having faith in others. Thomas Edison was sent home from school because his teacher said he was hopeless. Years later he wrote: "I won out because my mother never, for a single moment, lost faith in me."

MIRACLES

Work miracles by giving courage. Many ideas have failed to be realized because men lacked the courage to see them through. Promising careers have been abandoned because men were afraid. Cheer people on. Instill courage in their hearts.

Work miracles by rousing the imagination. You can never tell what will happen when you set a man's mind on fire with a great dream or purpose. Mentor Graham, Lincoln's teacher, lighted a fire that made a President.

Work miracles by expecting great things. Men will rise to do the seemingly impossible to justify the high expectations you hold for them.

Work miracles by counselling patience. Many a man has turned and left the dock just before his ship came in. Stress the wisdom of working and waiting. Time has great power to solve problems.

Work miracles by setting a good example. Others will catch your spirit! The power of a good example is the greatest miracle-working power of all.

Work with God to inspire men to come alive to their infinite possibilities.

The Art of

The pen *is* mightier than the sword! The pen in your hand is a magic wand with which you can send joy, hope, love and courage across deserts and plains, over mountains and seas, around the world and around the corner . . .

Put your words in a letter. Spoken words die on the empty air. Words in a letter endure and can be read again and again.

Tell those you love that you love them—and tell them *now* while they are alive and eager for appreciation and praise. Send them love letters!

When families are scattered in many states, and in foreign lands, hold them together with letters.

Friends tend to fade away through neglect. Keep friendships alive with letters.

If you feel burned up with resentment and anger at someone, tell him off in a letter. Get rid of the venom, get it out of your system. *Then burn the letter!*

Young people need to be constantly encouraged to make the most of their lives. Letters serve as pats on the back to cheer them on.

The book that inspired you. The painting that warmed your heart. The music that thrilled you. Thank with letters those whose toil and devotion have enriched your life.

WRITING LETTERS

When someone wins an award, gives a speech, leads a drive, preaches an eloquent sermon, or contributes to the general good in any way, lift his spirit with a letter of congratulation.

The doctor who saved your life, who sat for long hours at your bedside. Write him a letter of gratitude for all he has done for you.

Letters are conveyors of ideas. Do you have a suggestion for your mayor, governor, congressman, senator, or the President of the United States? Don't just think it, for no one can read your mind. Put it in a letter and mail it. Letters make citizens articulate.

Keep a notebook handy in which to jot down thought-starters: experiences, adventures, happenings, good news, quotations, to put sparkle into your letters.

Collect cartoons, snapshots, items from newspapers and magazines that have special significance to people you know. Then tuck them in with your letters.

The coming of the postman is like the daily round of a Santa Claus. Your letters can be gifts to add a new glow to the lives of people.

All you need to write a letter is a pen, a piece of paper and *you*. Get into the envelope and seal the flap!

The Art of

Ashley Montagu, the anthropologist, defined education in these words: *"To nourish and cause to grow."*

The art of education is to continue to grow as long as you live.

Grow from what you are into what you desire to be. Live to learn and learn to live.

Grow a larger concept of education. Every moment brings its lesson. Every person is a teacher. Every place is a schoolroom. Your university is the universe.

Grow in all directions. Cultivate the whole man. Develop a desire for goodness, an eagerness for knowledge, a capacity for friendship, an appreciation of beauty, a concern for others . . .

Grow in your love of learning. "Love is ever the beginning of Knowledge, as fire is of light," wrote Carlyle.

Grow an inquisitive mind. Remember the Chinese proverb: "He who asks a question is a fool for five minutes; he who does not ask a question is a fool forever." You can learn from everyone and everything.

EDUCATION

Grow in awareness. Keep the channels of your senses alert to all that goes on outside of you. Keep your mind alert to the stream of thought received within you.

Grow in new directions. Do not stagnate in the backwash of outworn tradition. Respect the past and learn its lessons, then be alive to inquiry and change. Explore new areas and ideas.

Grow in the deeper levels of the human spirit: contemplation, insight, intuition and prayer. "Spirit," wrote Bernard Eugene Meland, "rises out of the structures of consciousness that are receptive to the vision of good."

Grow in wisdom and understanding. Remember this secret from that ancient Chinese volume, *The Book of Changes:* "Every human being can draw in the course of his education, from the inexhaustible wellspring of the divine in man's nature."

Grow through all your years. Take inspiration from Michelangelo, who created works of art unequaled by any other man and yet, in his ninetieth year, regretted that he must die just when he was beginning to learn the ABC's of being a sculptor and painter.

Grow! Man is never finished. Man never arrives. Education never stops.

The Art of

The key to the art of prayer is thought. As we think so we pray.

The highest level of prayer is to think God's thoughts after Him, to attune our lives to love, hope, faith, justice, kindness; to become open channels for the goodness of God.

Prayer is quiet meditation about eternal values. It is the mind adventuring in the universe. Prayer moves with the instantaneous speed of thought, through infinite space, to the four corners of the earth, to the depth of the human heart, to the mountaintop of aspiration . . .

Prayer is a cup held high to be filled. It is an inward quest for inspiration. It is mentally reaching out for the great thoughts and illuminations of man in his continual search for meaning.

Prayer does not change God, it changes us. It deepens insight, increases intuitive perception, expands consciousness. It transforms personality.

Prayer opens doors to let in God and let out self, to let in love and let out hate, to let in faith and let out fear.

Prayer helps us to find ourselves. By praying not to get more, but to *be* more, we discover a way to serve, a purpose for which to live, a dream to make real.

PRAYER

Prayer brings God into our relationships with our fellow men. It applies spiritual perspective to the creative solution of human problems. We gain a wider awareness of the needs of others and a wiser knowledge of how to respond.

Prayer helps us to find the way, just as a hunter lost in the woods climbs a tall tree to get his bearings.

Prayer is thinking and thanking. It is thinking of our many blessings and accepting them with a thankful spirit.

Prayer works in the mind as a healing force. It calms the patient, enlightens the physician, guides the surgeon, and it often victoriously applies the power of the spirit when all seems lost. It proves, over and over again, the truth of Tennyson's words: "More things are wrought by prayer than this world dreams of."

Prayer puts us on God's side. It aligns us with life's highest purposes, aims and ideals.

Prayer is power always available. In *The Practice of the Presence of God,* Brother Lawrence said that even amidst the clatter of pots and pans in the monastery kitchen, "I possess God in as great a tranquility as when on my knees."

Prayer is dedicating our thought, feeling and action to the expression of goodness. It is to become like a window through which the light of God shines.

The Art of

Good citizenship is a personal thing. The good citizen reaches out to others with an open hand, an open mind and an open heart. He sees the potential bigness in little people. He lifts people up instead of letting them down.

Good citizenship calls for action. The good citizen gets off the side lines and takes part in the struggle. He recognizes that humanity moves forward not only from the mighty shoves of its great leaders but also from the tiny pushes of the rank and file of the people. He uses the humble ounces of his weight to help tip the scale for what he thinks is right.

Good citizenship applies the power of the ballot. The good citizen uses his vote as a flaming sword to crusade for the kind of city, state, nation and world in which he wants to live.

Good citizenship begins at home. The good citizen observes the law. He helps to keep his city clean. He keeps his house painted, his lawn trimmed and flowers growing in his garden. He champions worthy causes and helps the unfortunate. He strives to be

GOOD CITIZENSHIP

a good neighbor and to do well the thousand and one little things that add up to the big things we all want.

Good citizenship calls for balanced living in the vital areas of work, play, love and worship. The good citizen strives to do his daily work well and thus contribute to human happiness. He takes time to play and to laugh and to look up at the stars. He makes his home and family the center of his activities and takes pride in being a good parent. He leaves room for the life of the spirit.

Good citizenship is built on faith. The good citizen has the daring of a great faith. He lifts his sights above doubt and fear. He believes in the possibilities of world peace and in a growing understanding and cooperation between men. He thinks, talks and lives in harmony with his faith.

The good citizen clings to his great expectations. Though defeat may come and dark clouds appear, he maintains a vibrant faith in the future of mankind.

The Art of

The art of joy is having a love affair with life.

It is embracing life, drawing close to you all the beauty and wonder and goodness of the universe.

It is having a heart aglow with warmth for all your companions on the journey of life.

It is an expression of inner music. It is radiating joy as does a band of musicians marching down the street.

It is a blend of laughter and tears. Often it is the deep joy that comes to you through the mist of the years as you recall tender memories of joyous days gone by.

It is sharing your joy. "Some people," wrote the poet Walt Whitman, "are so much sunshine to the square inch." The joyous person seems to be plugged in to the sun itself.

It is celebrating life. The Master turned water into wine that the joyous wedding feast might continue. "Be of good cheer," He said. He proclaimed the purpose of his message to men

JOY

in these words: "That my joy might remain in you and that your joy might be full."

It is the putting forth of all your powers. It is the flood-tide of inspiration, the glory of creation. As you work with joy you find joy in your work.

It is looking for the joys that come in small, precious packages and making the most of them, knowing that big packages of joy are few and far between.

It is making the most of now, enjoying what is at hand. It is taking time to enjoy life as you go along.

It is an awareness of the heaven that exists all about you. As Solomon said: "He that hath a bountiful eye shall be blessed." It is making each day your most wonderful day.

Joy is the flag you fly when the Prince of Peace is in residence within your heart.

Joy is love bubbling forth into life.

The Art of

A man thinks in word-symbols, and such silent thought is equivalent to talking to himself. Sometimes when he is alone he speaks the words aloud. But silent or aloud, his conversation with himself is creative . . . it makes him what he is.

More important than what others say to him is what he says to himself. A man's life is shaped by the way he habitually talks to himself.

A man can talk himself up or down, into happiness or unhappiness, into failure or success, into heaven or hell.

When he talks to himself in words of self-pity, defeat, cynicism, futility, fear, anxiety, despair, hopelessness and resignation, he tears himself apart and shatters his future.

A man can transform his life by switching the emphasis of his inner conversation to words that lift and inspire.

He can talk strength into his backbone so he will have the courage and confidence to stand up to life.

He can talk himself out of discouragement and despair by counting his many blessings.

TALKING
TO YOURSELF

He can talk himself into accepting hardships and handicaps and enduring them with a gallant spirit.

He can talk himself into seeing his duties and responsibilities in a new light—as opportunities and privileges.

He can talk himself into having a new faith in the love of God and the greatness of men.

He can talk to himself about the beauty, glory and wonder of life so it will glow with a new radiance.

He can talk to himself about his dreams, hopes and aspirations. He can convince himself that there is a place for him and an important work for him to do.

The way a man talks to himself has a dynamic power for self-influence. His words can make or unmake his life.

"Nobody," wrote Cicero, "can give you wiser advice than yourself."

The Art of

Without the power to decide, a man's thoughts and dreams are like vapor blown in the wind. He goes nowhere until he decides where to go.

Life is made up of little decisions and big decisions, and how a man decides determines the direction of his life.

Decision is the spark that ignites action. Until a decision is made nothing happens.

Decision is the courageous facing of issues, knowing that if they are not faced problems will remain forever unanswered.

Decision does not straddle the fence. It takes a firm stand on one side or the other.

Decision can lead to the mountaintop. It can also cause a man to fall to the valley below. But without decision no mountains are climbed.

Decision is often the difference between greatness and mediocrity. In every man's life there comes a time when he must search for a cause, a work, an ideal to which he can give himself. Whether he says "Yes" or "No" to the challenge will determine his future.

DECISION

Decision is the freeing of one's self from the morass of fear, doubt, anxiety and uncertainty. It is the courage to risk a wrong decision rather than to make no decision at all.

Decision is not blind chance. It is focusing the powers of intelligence, meditation and prayer on the thing to be decided.

"We must make no important decision," wrote St. Ignatius Loyola, "without opening our hearts to love."

Decision need not always be made at once. Deciding to delay making a decision is a decision in itself. Many times it is best for one calmly and expectantly to "wait on the Lord" until more light comes.

Decision often concentrates resolve. A man decides on one great cause or mission as the motivation for his life. He says with St. Paul: "This one thing I do!"

Decision awakens the spirit of man. It gives him a goal, a purpose, a reason for being alive. Once a major decision is made, carrying it out becomes a matter of will and courage and dedication. The great decision comes first, the great work follows.

Decide now who and what you will serve. Decision is the first step toward going somewhere.

The Art of

Great men are little men expanded. Great lives are ordinary lives intensified. *All lives are potentially great.*

The art of the great life is marked by emphasis on qualities like these...

It is great to love life. Accept life as a precious gift from the hand of God and strive to make the most of it.

It is great to serve life. The most important thing in life is not what people can do for you but what you can do for people. Lose yourself in a cause bigger than yourself.

It is great to be alive to the best in life. To be alive only to material possessions and goals is to live in the shallows. Launch out into the deep where the treasures are!

It is great to stand for something. Men of principle are the principal men. Character is the bedrock of true greatness.

It is great to seek excellence. Aspire to excel in your chosen work. Adopt the creed of the maker of the immortal Stradivarius violins. Perfection consists not in doing extraordinary things but in doing ordinary things extraordinarily well.

THE GREAT LIFE

It is great to have a free mind. Break down the walls of prejudice, fear and limitation. Have the courage to think your own thoughts, speak your own mind and live your own life.

It is great to be gentle. The Chinese philosopher Lao-tze listed gentleness as the first quality of greatness. In an age of push use the magnetic pull of gentleness.

It is great to have creative zest. Have a sense of wonder and curiosity about the world. Have the boundless energy to explore, adventure and experiment with new ideas.

It is great to have great aims. Follow the counsel of Daniel Burnham: "Make no little plans; they have no power to stir men's blood. Make big plans, aim high in hope and work, remembering that a noble, logical diagram, once recorded, will never die."

It is great to keep open to the power of the Infinite. As a huge dam converts the power of a mighty river to create electricity and put it to work, so you can convert the golden river of God's goodness into *spiritual electricity* to help light the world.

It is great to multiply greatness. Feed other minds and help them to grow. Guide them in the art of discovery. Inspire others to live great lives.

63

About the Author

Wilferd A. Peterson was born in Whitehall, Michigan, and spent his boyhood in Muskegon. He is a former Grand Rapids advertising executive and in 1963 received the Silver Medal Award as advertising man of the year.

Mr. Peterson is the author of the best-selling The Art of Living *and* The New Book of the Art of Living. *He is a contributor to* This Week *Magazine and to* Reader's Digest *and writes a monthly page for* Science of Mind *Magazine. He also lectures on the Art of Living.*